DIFFERENT BUT THE SAME

Different but the same

James Omolo

Published by James Omolo, 2022.

While every precaution has been taken in the preparation of this book, the publisher assumes no responsibility for errors or omissions, or for damages resulting from the use of the information contained herein.

DIFFERENT BUT THE SAME

First edition. January 4, 2022.

Copyright © 2022 James Omolo.

ISBN: 979-8224059973

Written by James Omolo.

James Omolo

JAMES OMOLO

Once upon a time, there were two best friends, a caterpillar and a snail. They liked doing things together. One day they decided to go to a party that was outside their garden and they had to cross over a fence. The caterpillar went under the fence but the snail got stuck because its shell is too big...

So the snail tells the caterpillar that it can't get through and asks the
caterpillar to help by lifting the wire or build a little bridge to cross but

the caterpillar says, "Come on, just go under." But it was impossible for the snail to go under, his shell could not allow it....

The caterpillar insisted, come on....go under, we're going to be late for the party. The snail is getting frustrated because he doesn't want to be late for the party but the shell won't allow him as it is too big. The snail tells the caterpillar, I can't just crawl under the fence like you. So I really need your help. .....

The snail suggests that they could take a different route. The caterpillar
gets angry and tells the snail that the fact that he can crawl does not mean

he has it easy. 'Now I have a shell that makes it hard for me to go under the fence. So it is easier for you and harder for me', says the snail. They talked and after some time, they agreed and took a different route to the other side of the fence. Even though the route they took was a longer one, they went together and managed to get to the party.

Dad: Just like the story of caterpillar and snail, there are struggles that we go through that may be surprising for other people. We can learn from the story that even when we have trouble understanding each other, we can still come to an agreement and live happily side by side. We can disagree respectfully without hate. Everyone's struggle is different.

The reason I'm telling you this is because there are a lot of things going on in the world. I won't lie to you, there are things that people will say that are not good. I need you to try to be open and discuss them with me because I need you to always be prepared.

Some people are called white while others are called black but this is confusing. Look at this paper, its colour is white, does it look like the colour of your mum's skin? People who share the same colour as your mum are called white even though they don't look like the real shade of white. Now look at this colour on my shirt, it is black, is this the colour of my skin or yours? But people with my skin colour are called Black.

Being white or Black or brown is not just the skin colour, it's about our experiences within the society. Melanin makes us have different skin tones.

Those with a lot of melanin have darker skin, while ones with less melanin have lighter skin.

We look different outside but inside we are all the same. Isn't that amazing? So now, Black is a race and white is a race, remember, we are a human race but we have to talk about race because it affects our everyday life.

We are all human and nothing will change that, even the colour of our skins.

There are times that people will judge you for what (they think) you are not just because you have a different colour of the skin as theirs. Be happy with who you are. No matter what they say, it is possible to live with difficult emotions like anger, sadness, discomfort and still continue to move ahead and show compassion, kindness and hope.

Do not be afraid to get to know

others and learn even at a time

when you experience fear.

Try to understand why that person has a different world view than yours.

Dad: There are so many differences in the world. There are different people who believe different things and behave in different ways. There is as much diversity even within a group of people with the same skin colour. "Isn't it wonderful that we are all so different?" Our ancestors came from different places in the world and that's the reason we look different, speak different languages and even dress different.

Look in the mirror and love what you see!" What makes you different makes you great.

Daughter: Just like rainbow, it is beautiful because it has got many colours.

Dad: That's right my daughter. I tell you what, some people say they do not see colour, but that is not true. The reality is that nature has given us different colours and that makes everything beautiful. The sky is blue, the trees are green, even flowers, animals and birds have different colours and that makes everything unique and beautiful.

We should embrace our uniqueness and identity. Society will always try to choose for you your identity; people will makecomments or jokes to your face. Therefore it is important to speak out and to resist being silent.

When someone becomes mean to you or treat you unfairly, stand firm and say "I don't like that, "that's not kind", or "that's not true".

Read books with stories from different cultures, communities and traditions so that you will learn about them. Reading these stories will also teach you that we can celebrate our differences and discover our common humanity.

Look at this box of crayons and find a colour that you believe to be yourself. You will notice that there are different colours but the pencils and crayons are just the same. It's just a different crayon because of the different colour. Just like the crayons in the box, that is how we are, different but the same.

When someone thinks that one colour or race is better than another and treat others unfairly because of that belief, that is racism. It is a form of discrimination. Like calling other people names or physically attacking them. Racism causes great harm to people, that's why we have to talk about it and stand up against it.

Dad: You know what, most of the time when I'm in a public space, I notice that people are staring me a lot because I look different from them. Have you experienced the same thing when you are with other children at school or during your football matches or trainings?

Son: Yes, in many occasions.

Tell me one thing that worries you or makes you feel uncomfortable, scared, angry or sad?

Son: In school, children sometimes make fun of me being different.

We live in a world that continues to organize people along racial lines. There are words that some people use against Black people. You may have heard some of them especially in Poland where they use a terrible word called Murzyn. It is a powerful insult used to treat Black people as less human.

Dad: you are perfect blend of White and Black that's why you are perfect the way you are. Be proud of who you are and what you look like. Love yourself just the way you are and be your true self.

We are different in unique ways and beautiful in different ways. Don't be afraid of others, accept them. Get to know what makes their opinions about the world different from yours. Remember, our differences should not divide us.

Dad: I want you to know who you are and as you grow older, you will realize that people will treat you differently because of the colour of the skin. They may see you as something else. Therefore it is very important to love who you are but remember that even though you are both Black and white, you may not be able to use both sides to your advantage. It's important to be happy within. I just want you to understand that.

Dad: You know, some mommies and children share the same skin colour but other mommies have a different skin colour, did you know that?

I want you to remember white features and hair are not the standard by which we measure ourselves.

You and your brother are special, but other people are different and special too and that's what makes us human.

Mum: For you daughter how is it for you to look at your mum and see my skin colour is not the same as yours, my hair is also not the same as yours? How does that make you feel?

Daughter: Mum, it is Okay with me because I have half of you and I have half of daddy and I want to be both of you not only one of you.

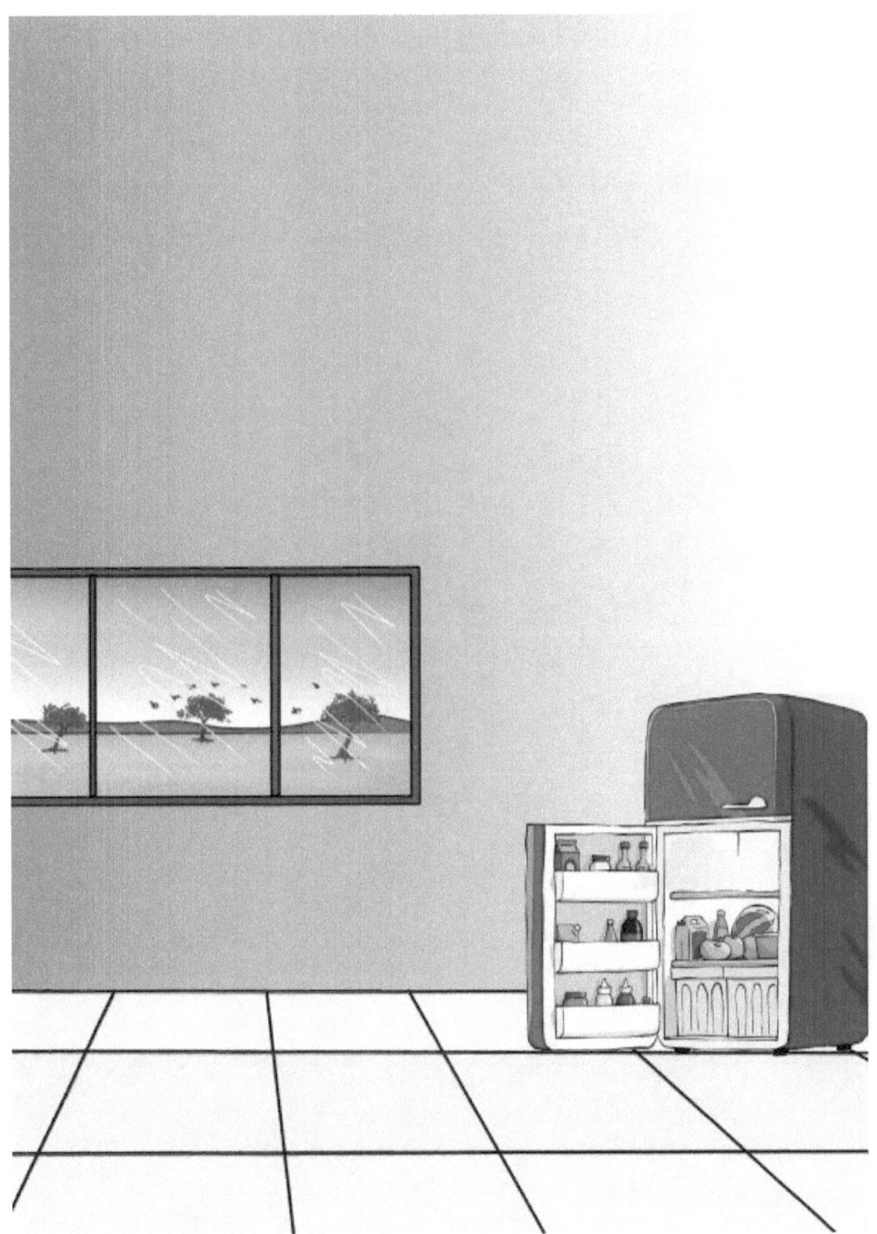

What I heard you say was...you like being mixed?

Daughter: Yes dad. I did not choose to be mixed, I just got lucky.

Dad: I love that.

Dad: You know, I am asking you because most people say that being mixed is confusing because they do not know where they belong or how to identify themselves because white people do not see them as white and sometimes Black people do not see them as fully Black. In fact the reality is that not everyone will see you as mixed but simply as being Black in different countries or places and that you will have to experience injustices that come with being Black.

Daughter: Last week when you came to pick me up from school, I heard some children saying that you do not look like my mum...

Mum: Families come in all shapes, skin colours and sizes...Some mommies and their children have the same skin colour and some mommies and their children have different skin colour. Did you know that?

Listen, it will be bad for you to compare yourself with others features or hair with white friends because we are made in different and special ways.

Daughter: What should I do when someone make a racist joke?

Dad: Being mixed means somebody is going to make a joke about you or my culture. Sometimes they may not even know it. Some people will say you are half, when you are actually whole. Racist jokes are hurtful. It takes a lot of strength to stand up to a bully and I would like you to be strong and kind in doing it.

In fact, if you do not feel comfortable answering the questions, just tell them politely that you don't want to talk about it anymore, then move on. Remember, you do not owe anybody an explanation. You are not responsible for making other kids feel comfortable with themselves.

Son: Sometimes kids ask me what I am. It is annoying.

Dad: Tell them that I do not need to choose. You do not have to choose one over the other

I tell you what, you can identify the way you want, and nobody should choose it for you. You are your mom who is Polish and your dad who is Kenyan.

Son: Sometimes children call me different names like chocolate.

Dad: How do you feel about that?

Son: Sometimes it makes me feel bad but I really do not care because I know what I am. They can say whatever they want to say.

Dad: Even when they look at you as different, try demonstrate self-confidence and self-acceptance. Why stick to one flavour of ice cream if you can get a variety.

Dad: How would you feel if somebody do not accept you? How would you feel when children say they do not want to play with you because you are not like them?

Son: For me, it is fine even though not normal. They can say what they want to say but I know who I am and what I am and I am comfortable with myself. I do not care what they think about me.

Dad: I like that, high five!!

Daughter: I really do not care because I know I am as white as I am Black

Dad: I am very proud of both of you. It makes me happy to see that at your age you are really confident of who and what you are. It is my duty to help you make this confidence stronger because it will help you when other children start treating you badly because they see you are different from them. Remember skin colour does not define who we are or what we should be.

Mum: When I met your dad, I knew that we have different skin colour but I saw a human being and he felt the same and look, now we have two beautiful children that have both of us.

Dad: I agree 100%. Also remember the person who will have a problem with you, is the problem. You are just who you are and you do not have to change anything.

Son: Some children told me that I am not Polish and that I was not born in Poland, but I tell them that I have two countries in two continents and that is special.

Dad: There is a popular saying that 'do not judge a book by its cover', it is what's in the inside that matters. Children who ask that question are just trying figure that out. They think that being from Poland one has to look like them, but being from here means you can look many different ways and speak many different languages.

Daughter: Some girls in my class told me that I am Black...

Dad: Yes you are Black as you are white because you took after mummy and daddy and that makes you special just like other children. We are all special even when we look different. Your skin colour is exactly the colour it should be.

Son: I am happy when I am home but sometimes I feel sad when I am in school because I feel different from the rest. Other children sometimes do not want to play with me.

Daughter: My classmates make fun of my curly hair and skin tone. They are always touching my hair. You notice whenever I come home; my hair is always wild.

Dad: I totally understand how you feel. People also make fun of me sometimes. None of that should make you feel less confident in who you are. You are perfect the way you are.

When you hear other people make fun of you or call you names,
stand up with your head high and politely tell them that what they are

saying or doing is rude and offensive and that I am upset that you speak hatefully of people like me.

You are just right the way you are. Tell the kids to stop touching your hair. You remember that solarium you see next to our house? Women go there to get the kind of colour you have.

Mum: Remember, people will be curious. Don't be shy in sharing who you are with people. Say it proudly, sometimes when I am with you, people ask me if you are my kids because they look at the different skin colour and I am so proud to tell them that you are.

Dad: My daughter, you will deal with a lot of issues in life. Never allow anyone to tell you what a girl can and cannot do. You are equal to any boy.

Dad: You know what, in my entire life I have been speaking out against boys and men who say girls cannot do stuff. Son, I want you know that respect is earned and honour girls as your equals; always rooted in love, peace, non-violence and healthy ways of expressing yourself.

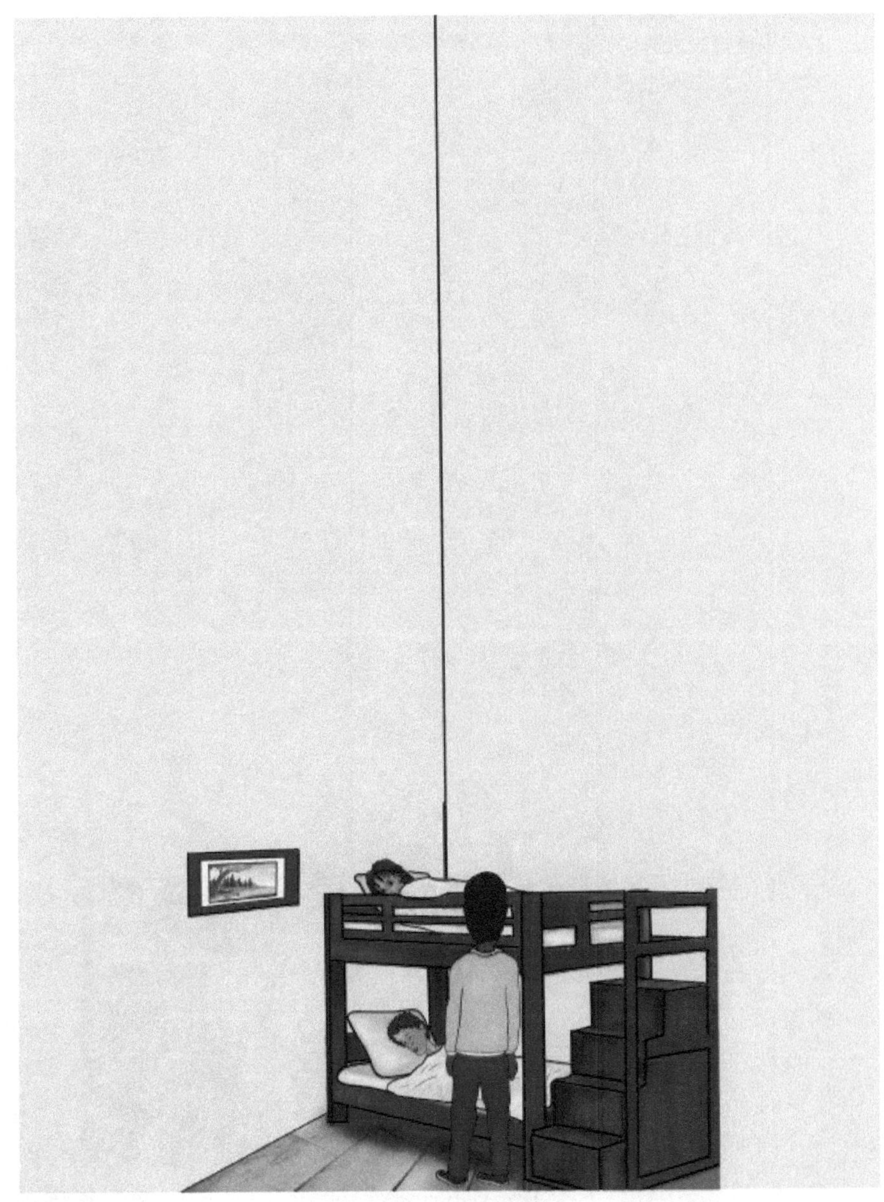

Dad: If someone openly express hate (and venom) towards you, respond with love always, remembering the need to keep a distance from the haters.

Dad: When you grow up, you are going to be what you want to be. Let nobody put you down. You have to be happy all the time because you are beautiful human beings. You hold your head up. Remember, sometimes, our experience may be different from someone else'. We may also see things different from other people's point of view. Sometimes you are the snail, sometimes you are the caterpillar. What's important is to understand that WE ARE DIFFERENT BUT THE SAME.

Edition published by
Cosmodernity Consultants
Copyright © 2021 by James Omolo
An imprint of Cosmodernity Consultants LLC

The snail and caterpillar story is courtesy of Franchesca Ramsey and Kat Blaque you
tube animation
(https://www.youtube.com/watch?v=hRiWgx4sHGg)
This book is co sponsored by Africancamera (www.africancamera.com)
Illustrations: Bob Odhiambo
Editing: Dominika Pasterska
First printing: 2021